DATE DUE

11-8-17									

T4-AEB-980

MONEY DOESN'T BUY HAPPINESS

And Neither Does Poverty

by

T. Alexander Anderson

TMPress, Inc.

COPYRIGHT © 2004 by TMPress, Inc.
All rights reserved. No part of this book may be used or reproduced
or transmitted in any form or by any means, electronic or mechanical, including
photocopying, recording, or by any information storage and
retrieval system, without written permission from the publisher.

Published by TMPress, Inc., 9256 Black Oaks Court, Maple Grove, MN 55311

TMPress books may be purchased for educational, business, or sales promotional use.
For information write TMPress, Inc., Marketing Department,
9256 Black Oaks Court, Maple Grove, MN 55311
e-mail: themoneybooks@hotmail.com
Printed by Ideal Printers, Inc., St. Paul, MN, U.S.A.

Library of Congress Cataloging-in-Publication data
Anderson, T. Alexander
Money doesn't buy happiness : and neither does
poverty / by T. Alexander Anderson. — 1st ed.
p. cm. - (The Money Books ; 2)
LCCN 2003097005
ISBN 0-9706856-2-9
1. Finance, Personal-United States-Humor
2. Quality of life-United States-Humor. I. Title.
HG179.A55983 2004   332.024'0207
QB103-200811
10 9 8 7 6 5 4 3 2 1

PREFACE

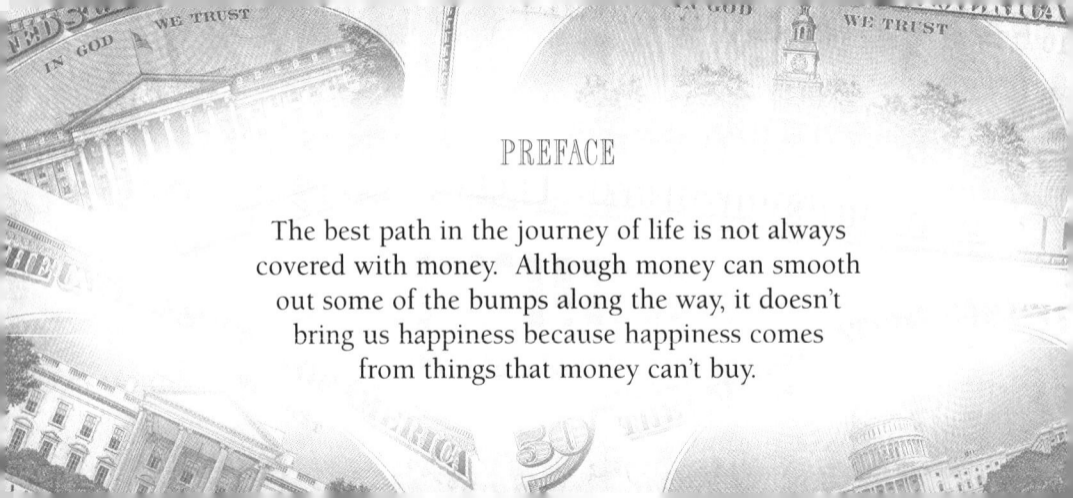

The best path in the journey of life is not always covered with money. Although money can smooth out some of the bumps along the way, it doesn't bring us happiness because happiness comes from things that money can't buy.

Money Doesn't Buy Happiness not only gives wisdom for greater happiness, it provides a foundation for true wealth. This book along with it's sister books, *Money Isn't Everything* and *It's Only Money*, may prove to be the best investments you ever make.

May you be happy and rich,
T. Alexander Anderson

FOR SCOTT

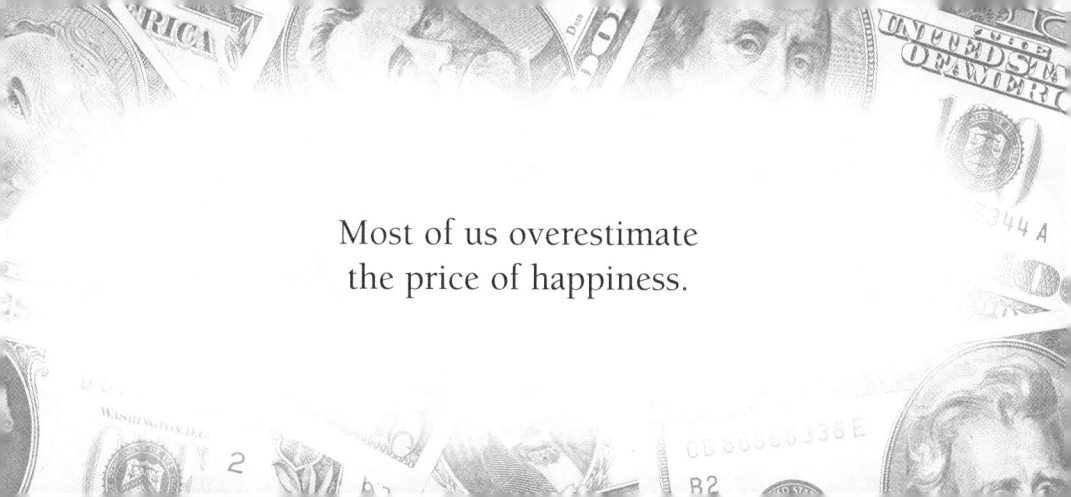

Most of us overestimate
the price of happiness.

Prosperity is a state of mind -
not a financial statement.

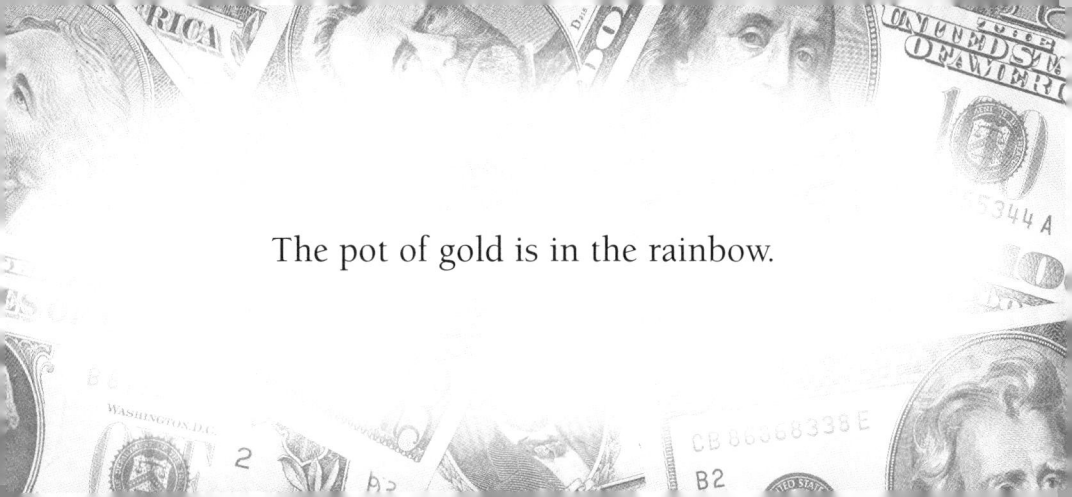

The pot of gold is in the rainbow.

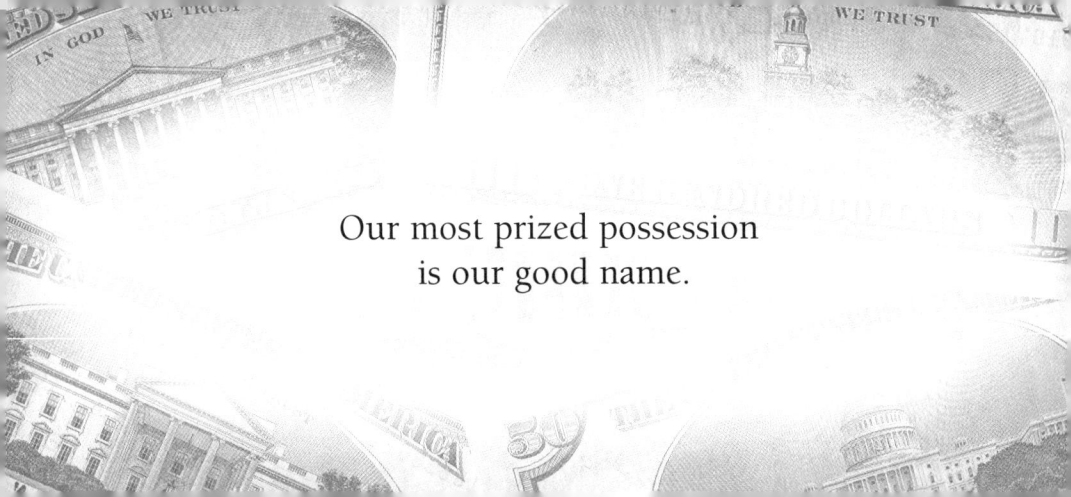

Our most prized possession
is our good name.

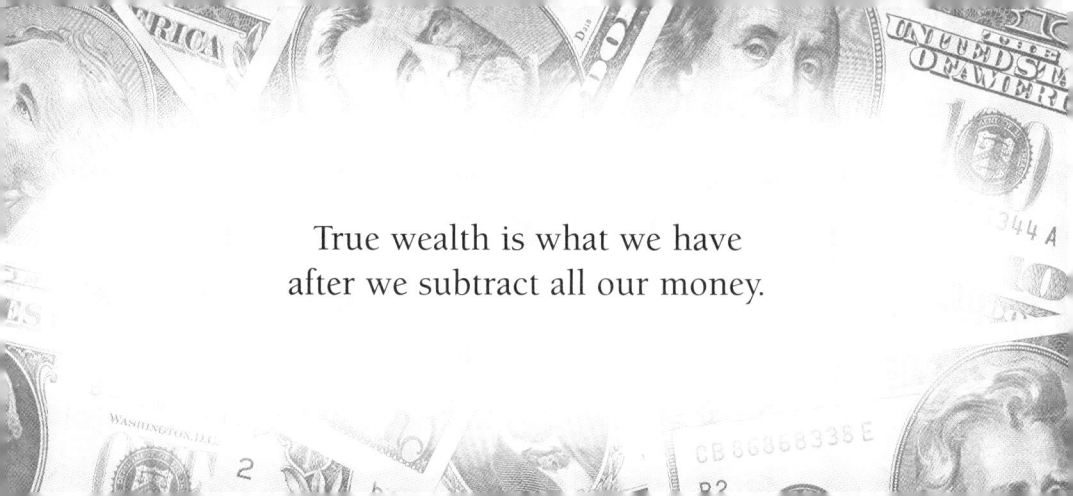

True wealth is what we have after we subtract all our money.

Money can be replaced - memories can't.

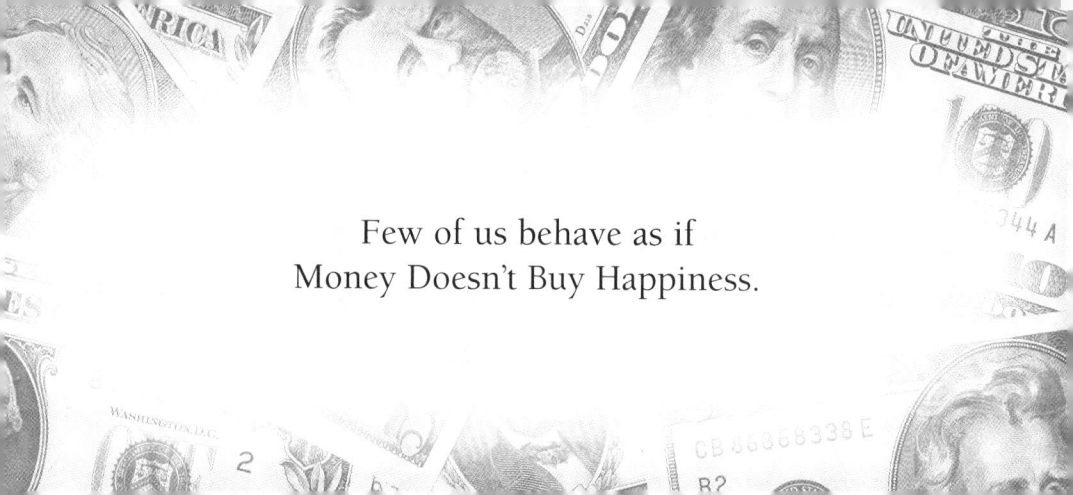

Few of us behave as if
Money Doesn't Buy Happiness.

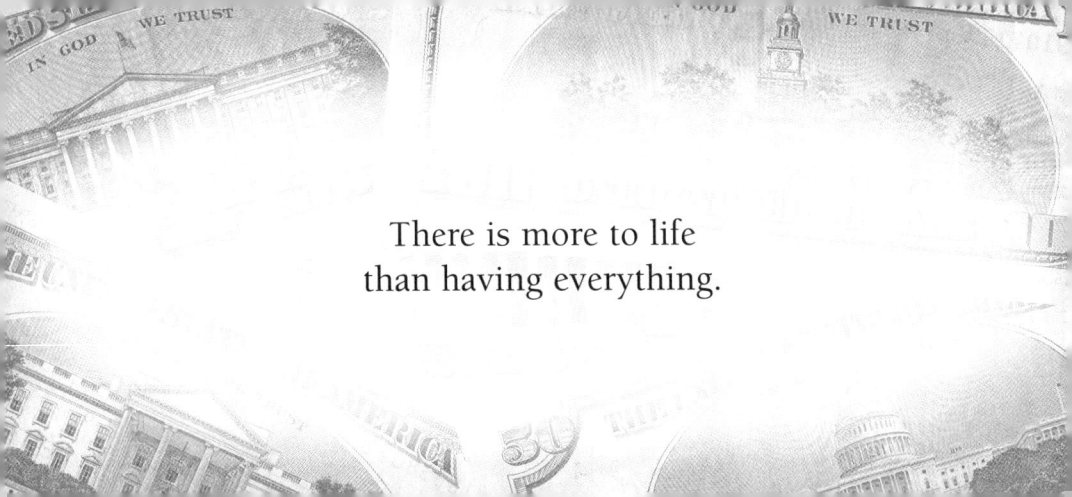

There is more to life
than having everything.

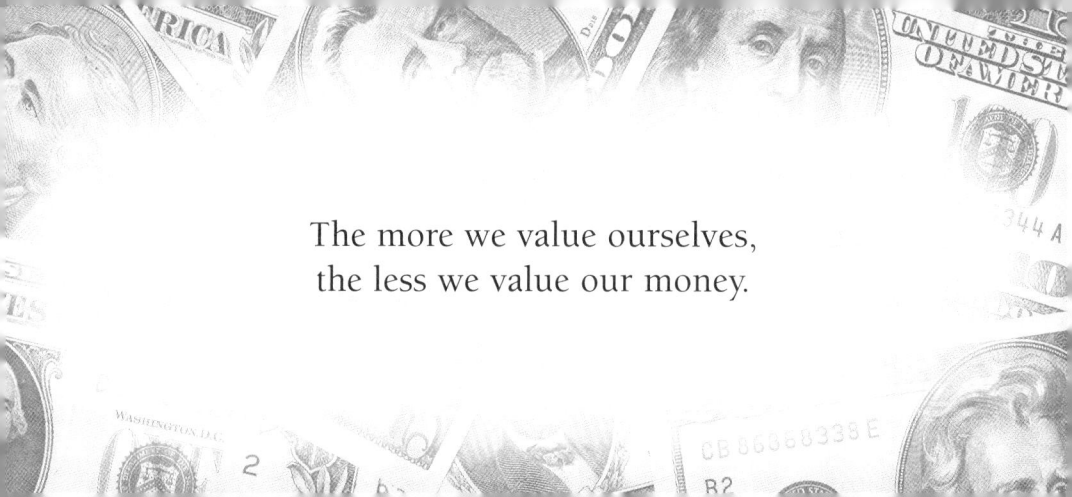

The more we value ourselves,
the less we value our money.

Time isn't money.
Time is priceless.

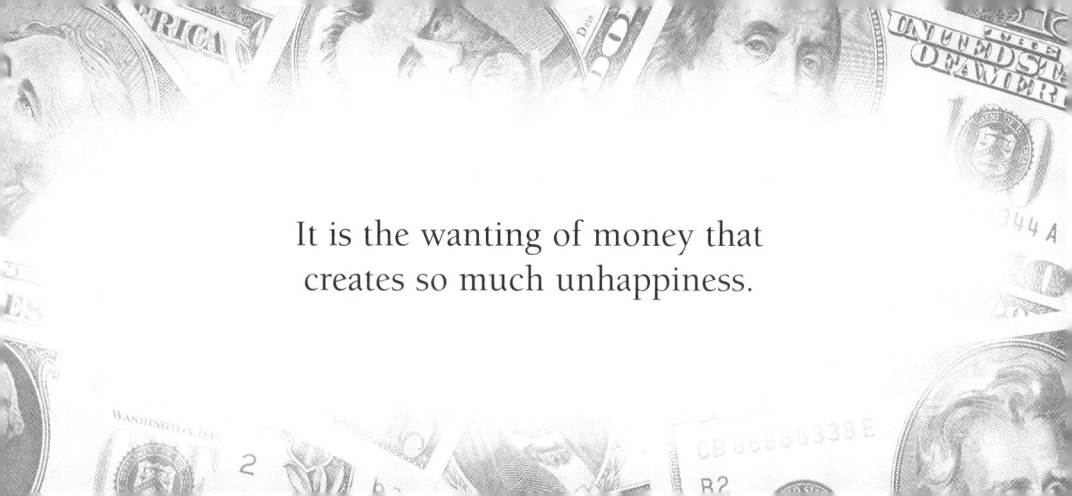

It is the wanting of money that creates so much unhappiness.

True needs are not conceived while shopping.

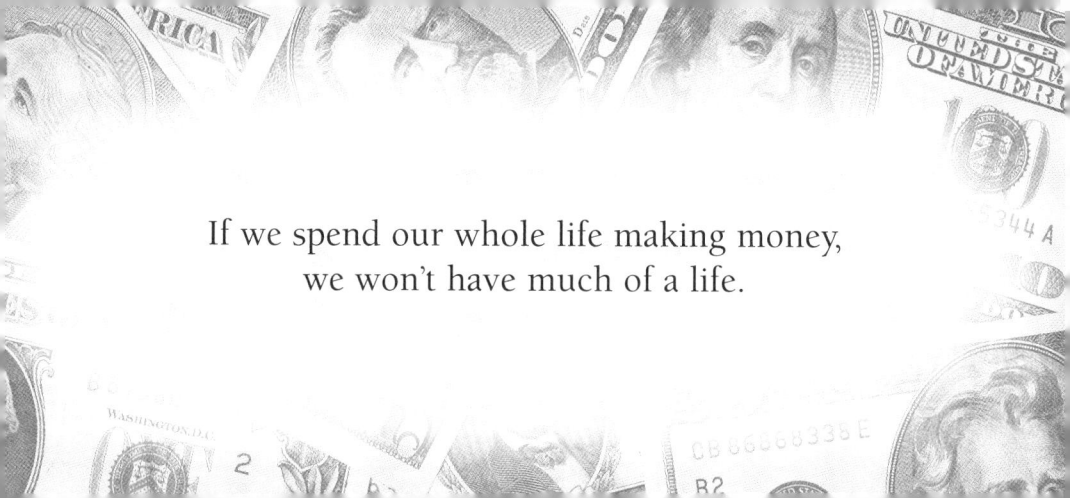

If we spend our whole life making money, we won't have much of a life.

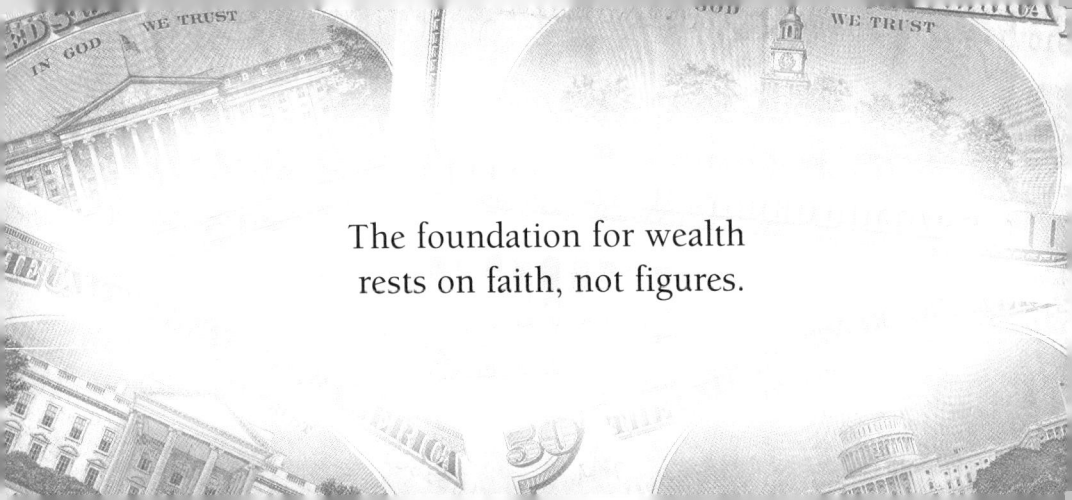

The foundation for wealth rests on faith, not figures.

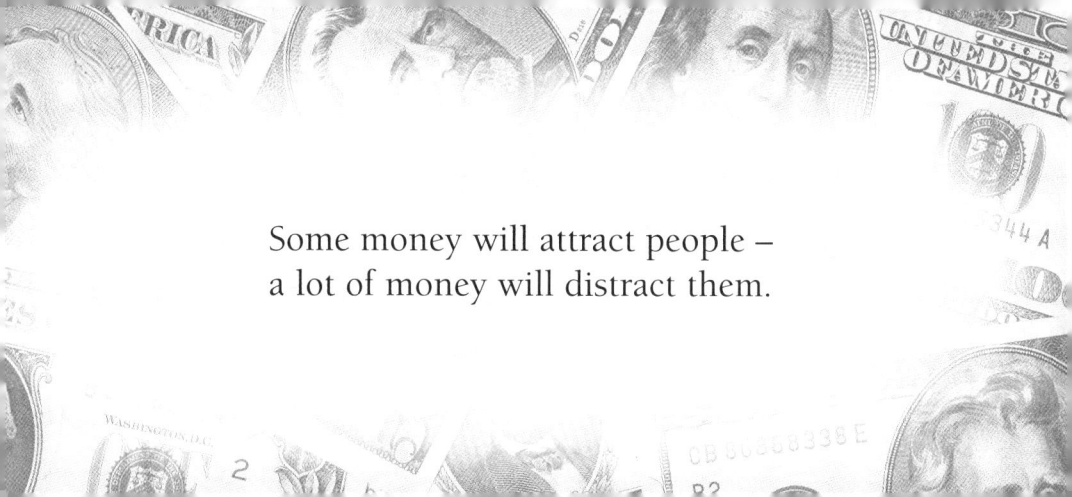

Some money will attract people – a lot of money will distract them.

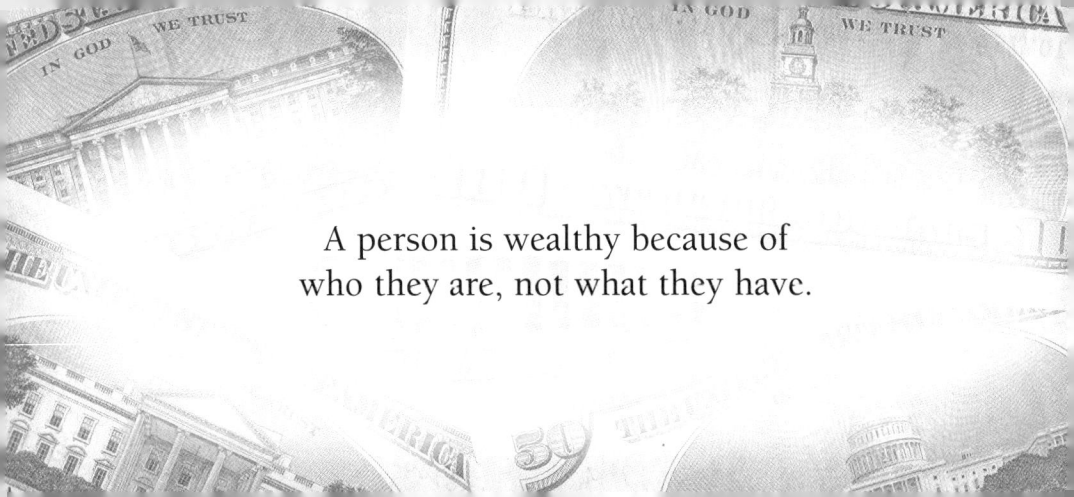

A person is wealthy because of who they are, not what they have.

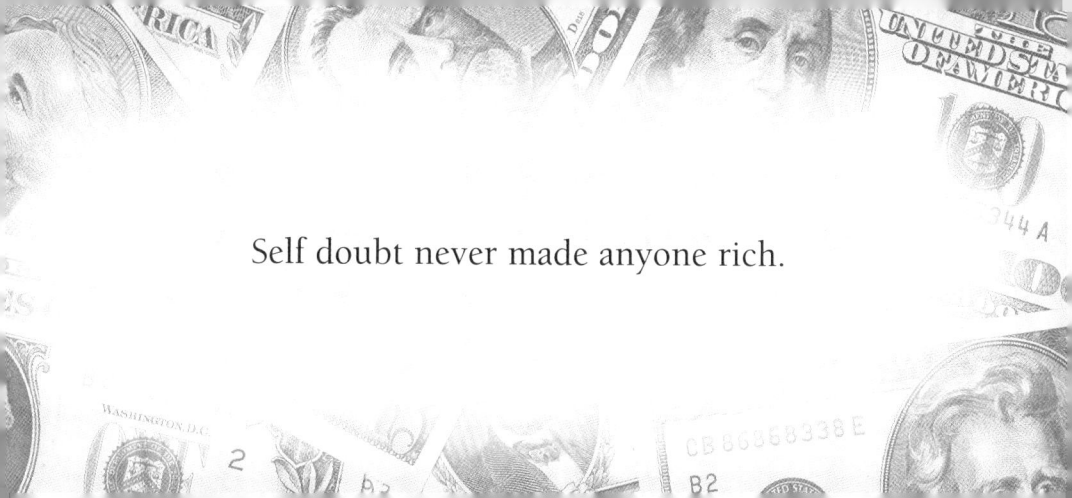

Self doubt never made anyone rich.

The more money our friends have,
the more expensive they are to be with.

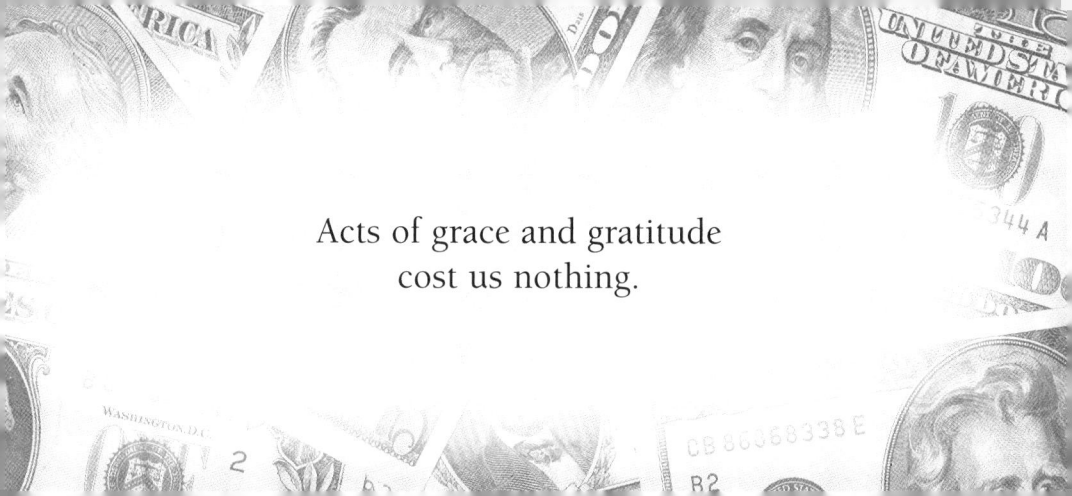

Acts of grace and gratitude cost us nothing.

Happiness consists not of having,
but enjoying.

The wealthiest people
know they can have anything they want
and realize they want nothing.

A person with a lot of money is not as rich as a person with a lot of knowledge.

Our relationship with money is often our most difficult.

We can't replace family time with money.

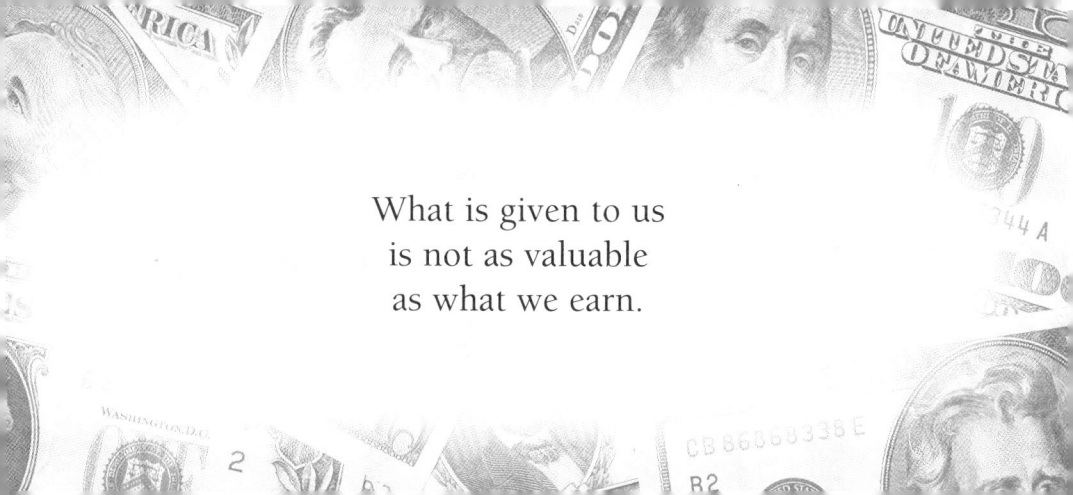

What is given to us
is not as valuable
as what we earn.

Our minds and bodies have no price tag.

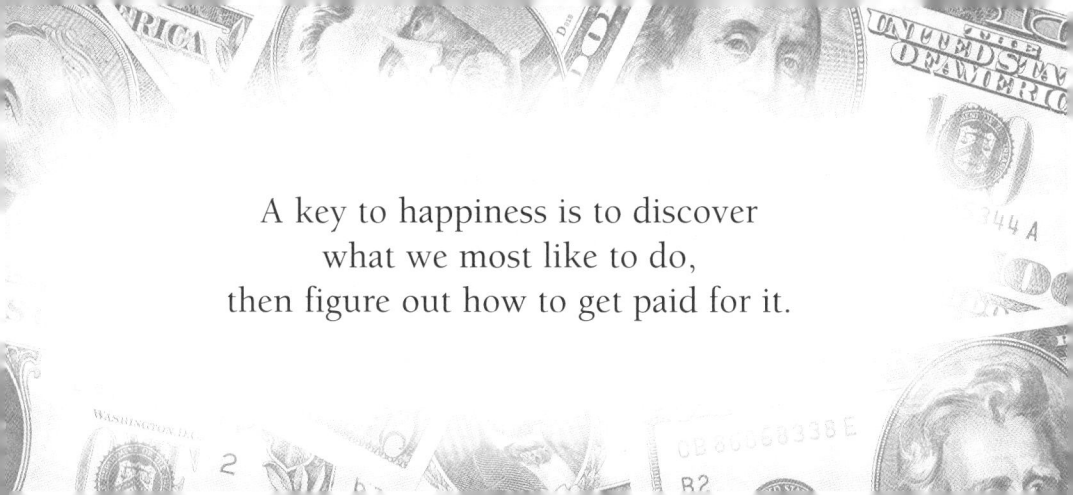

A key to happiness is to discover
what we most like to do,
then figure out how to get paid for it.

The most meaningful gifts
are not tax deductible.

Remember not to confuse
WEALTH with SUCCESS.

Adversity is a better teacher than Prosperity.

The least expensive way to improve our looks
is to smile.

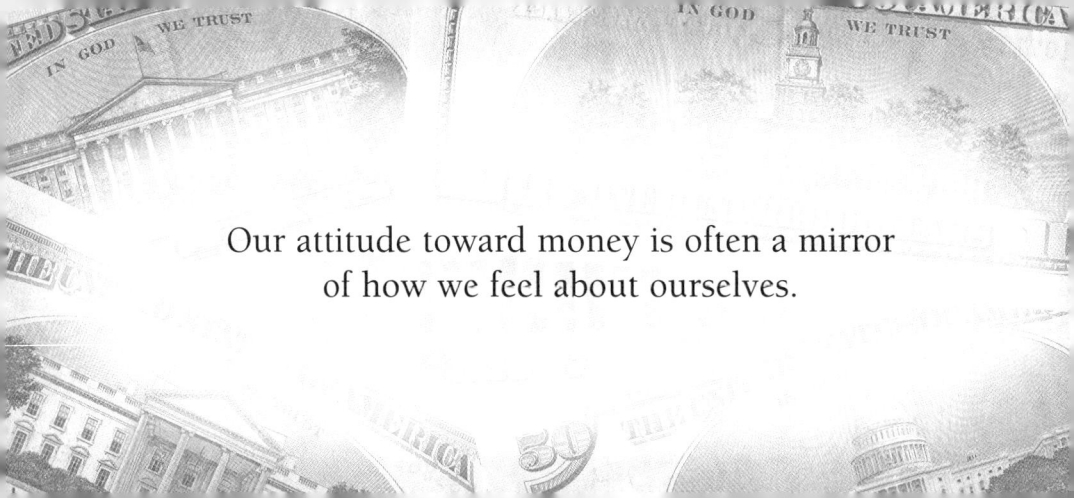

Our attitude toward money is often a mirror of how we feel about ourselves.

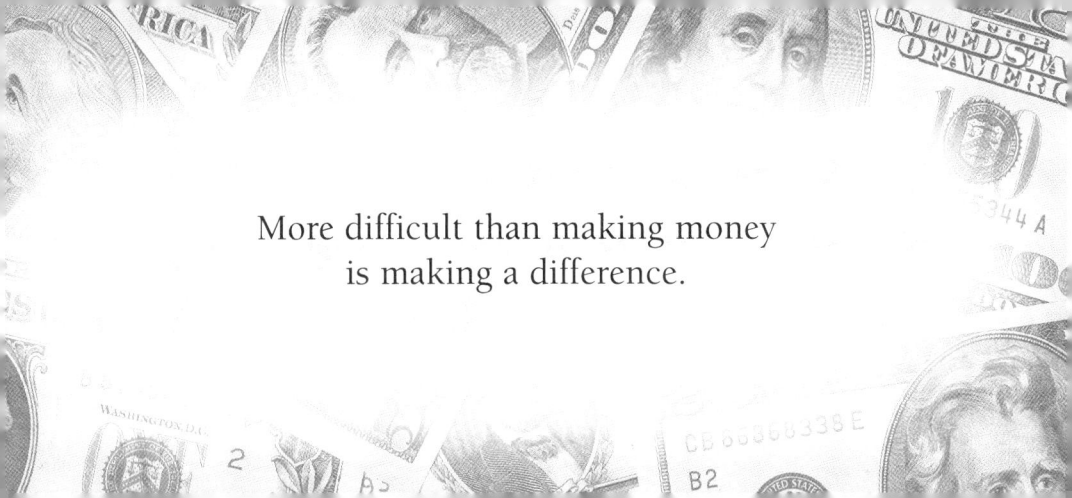

More difficult than making money
is making a difference.

Everyone should spend their money, at least once, on something that will outlast their life.

NET WORTH
does not equal
SELF WORTH.

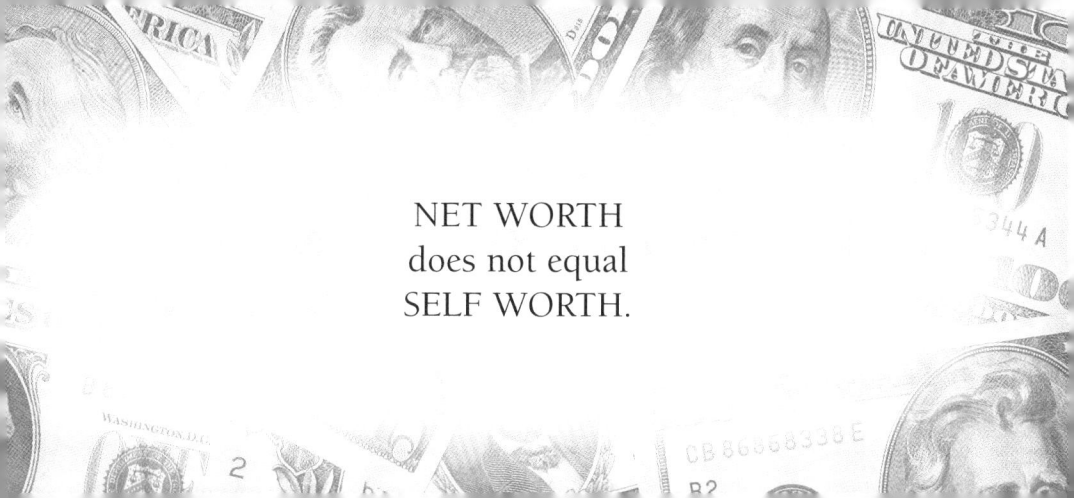

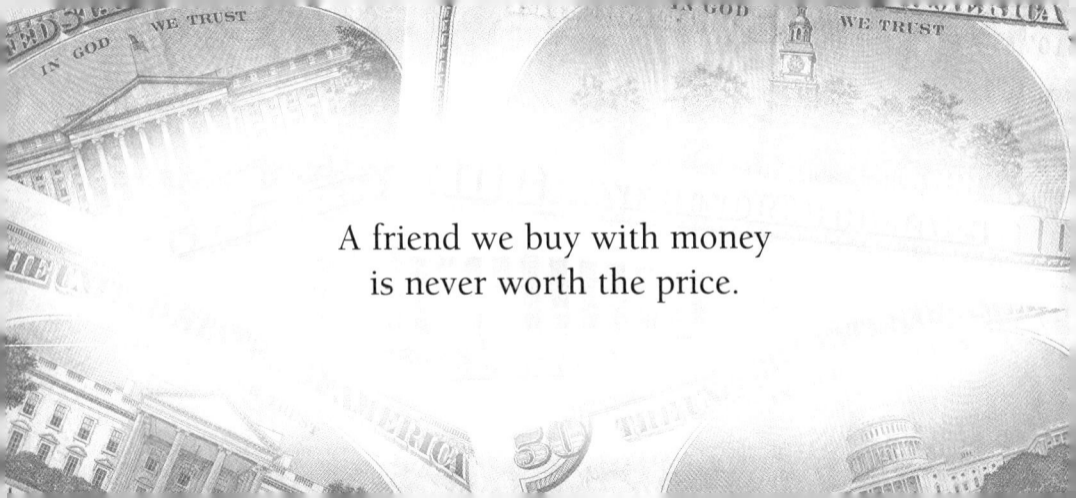

A friend we buy with money
is never worth the price.

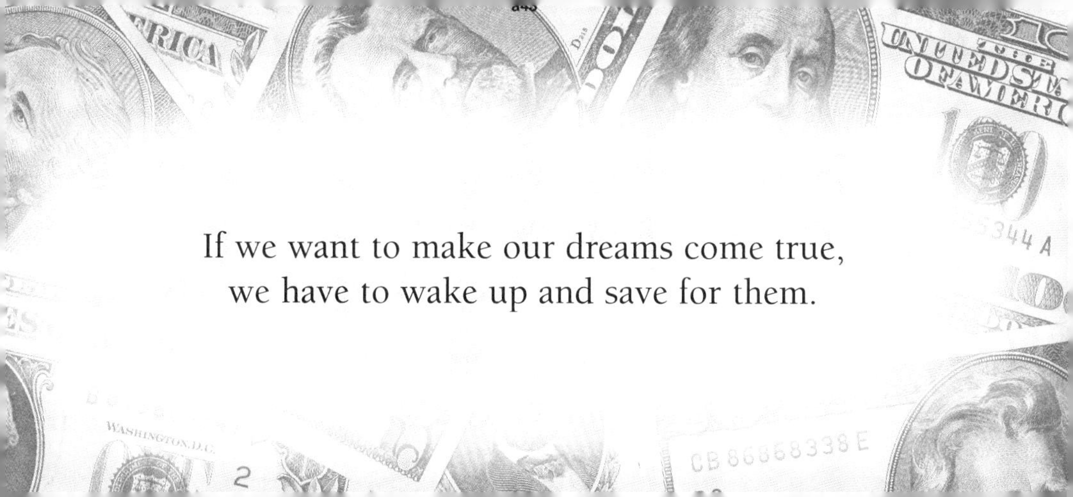

If we want to make our dreams come true,
we have to wake up and save for them.

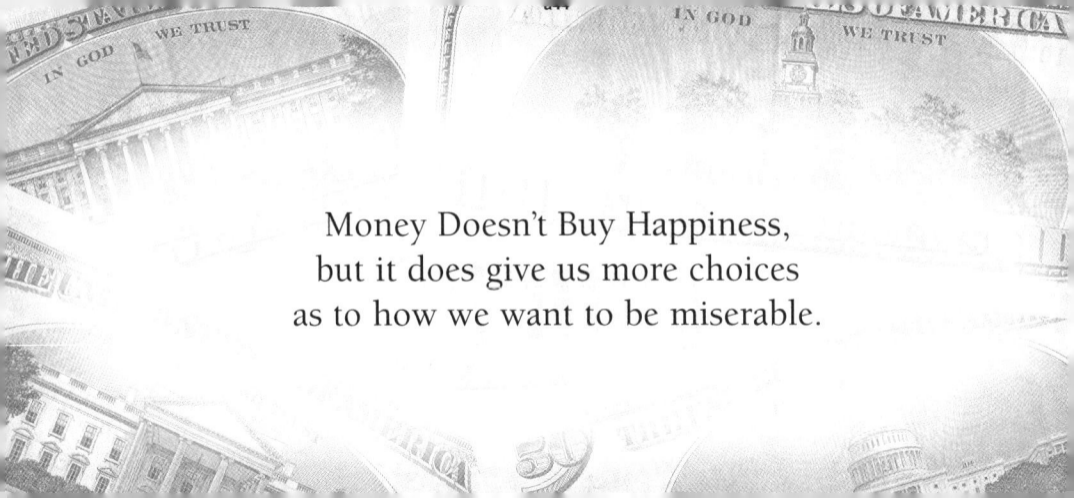

Money Doesn't Buy Happiness,
but it does give us more choices
as to how we want to be miserable.

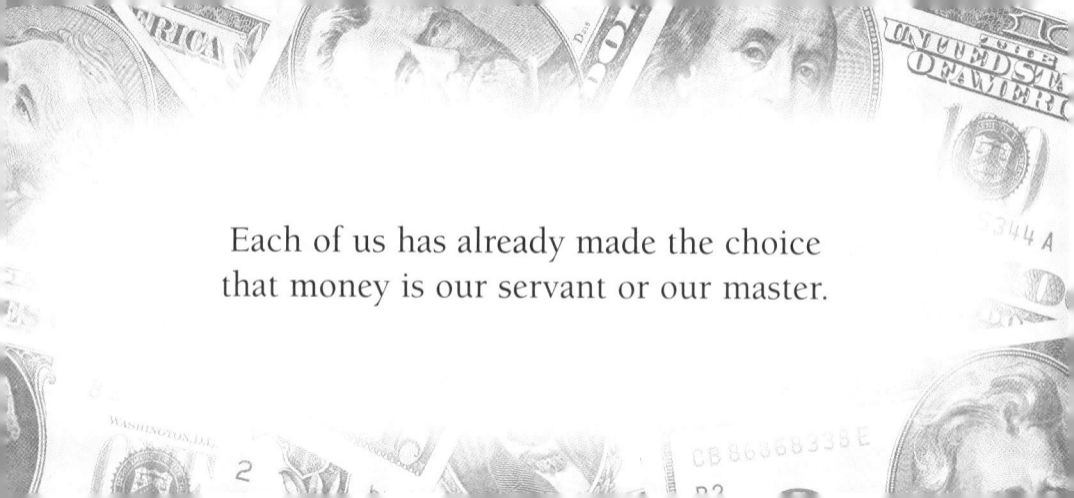

Each of us has already made the choice
that money is our servant or our master.

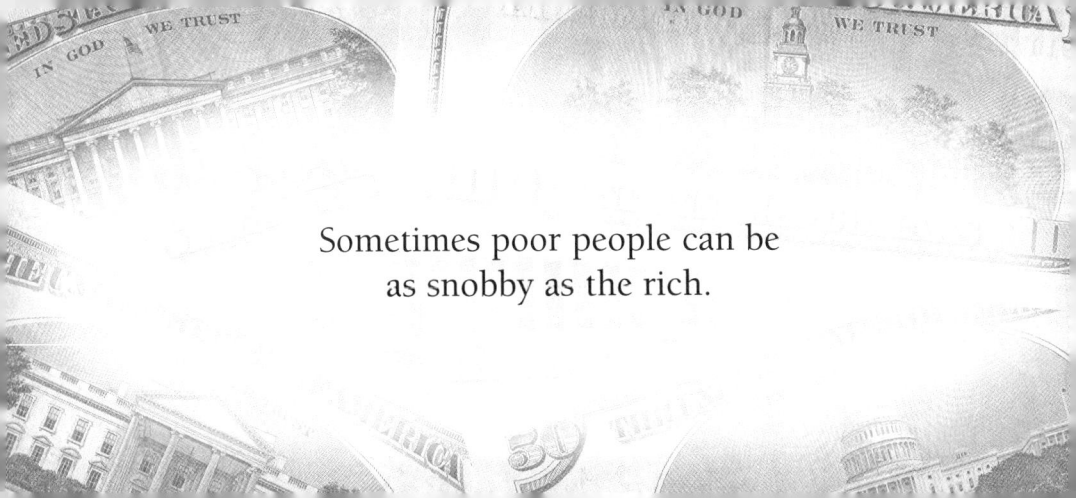

Sometimes poor people can be as snobby as the rich.

The purpose of life is not to make money.

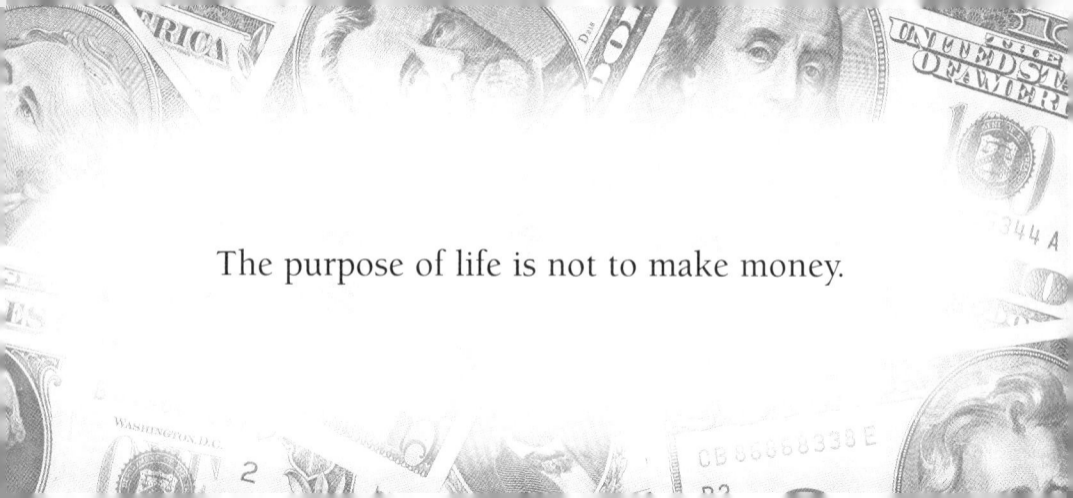

It is when we meet someone
who has no desire for money, power, or fame,
that we realize how poor we really are.

Money frees us from doing those things we don't like to do.

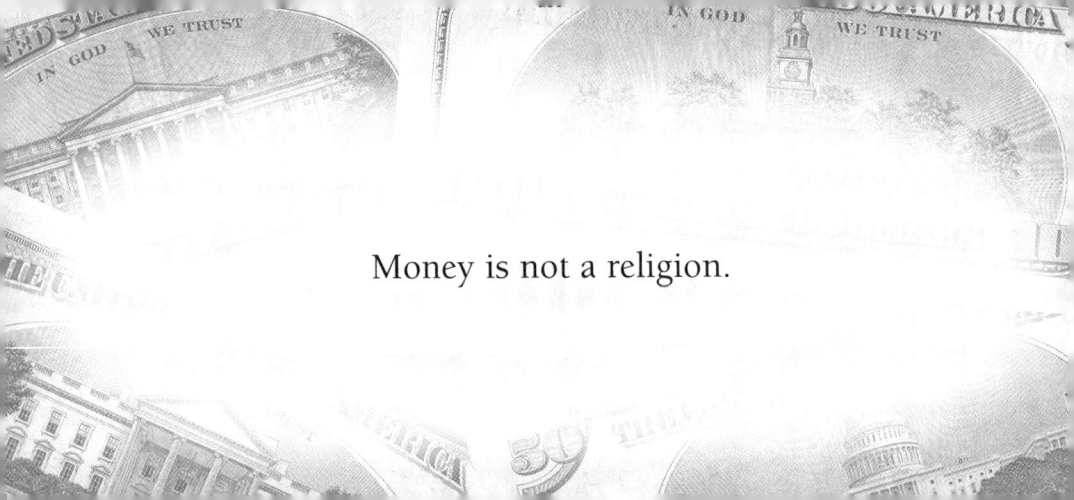

Money is not a religion.

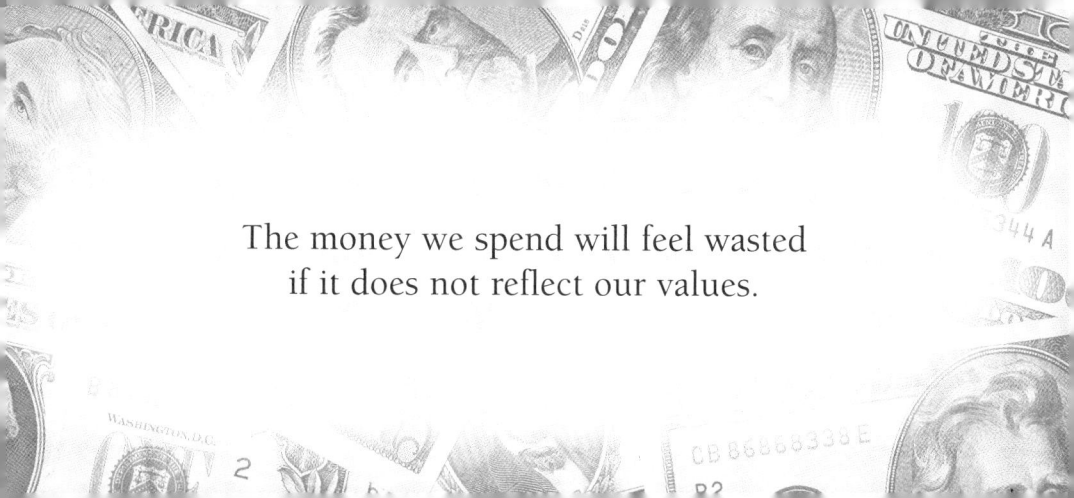

The money we spend will feel wasted
if it does not reflect our values.

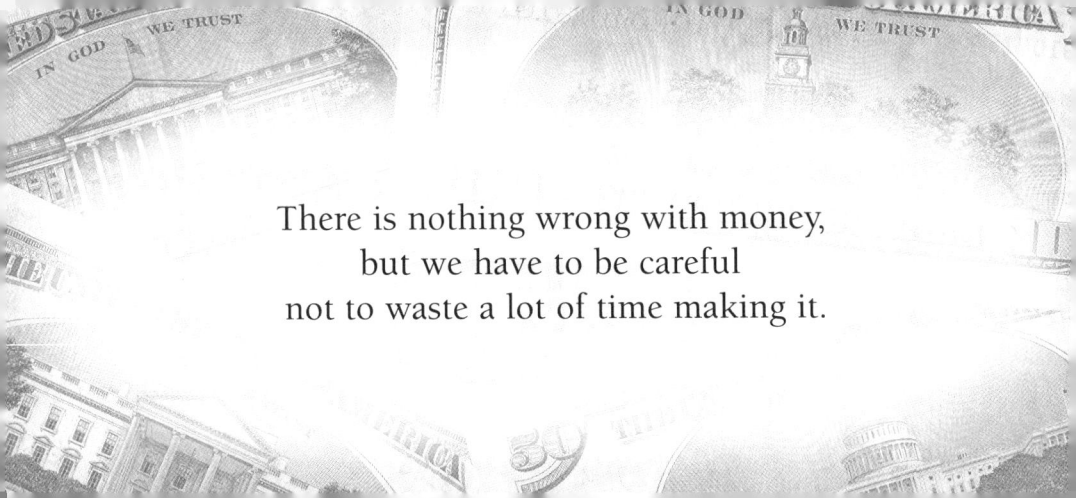

There is nothing wrong with money,
but we have to be careful
not to waste a lot of time making it.

We need to forget what we give,
and remember what we get.

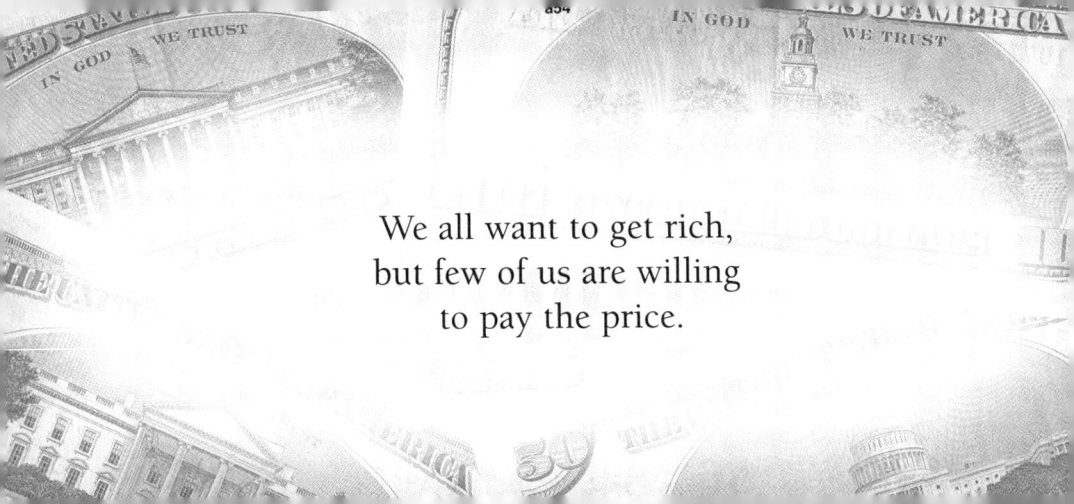

We all want to get rich,
but few of us are willing
to pay the price.

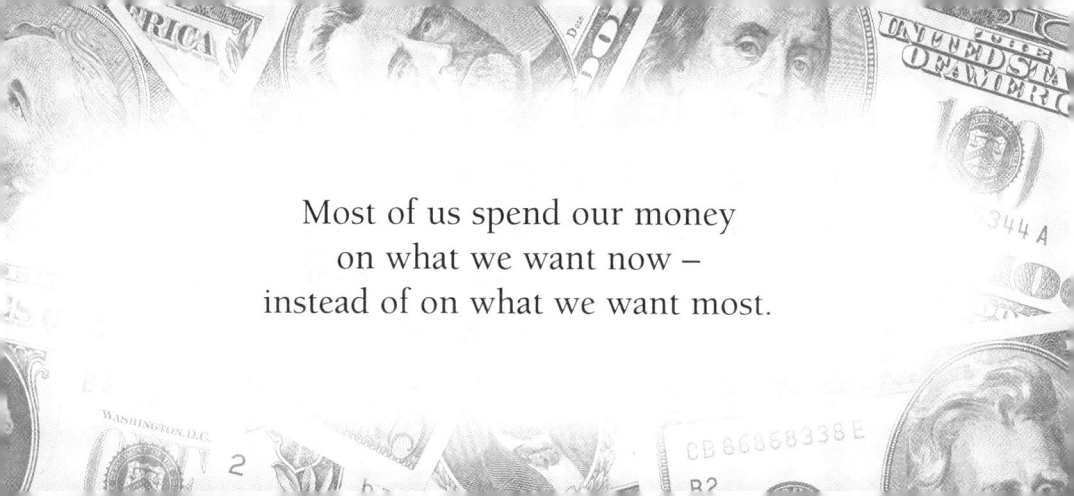

Most of us spend our money
on what we want now –
instead of on what we want most.

A status symbol is something we buy that we can't afford.

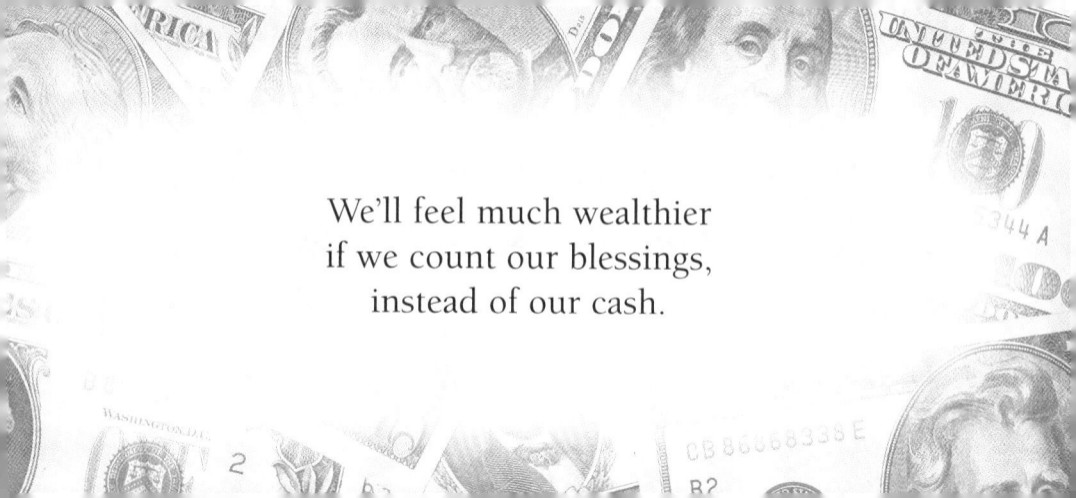

We'll feel much wealthier
if we count our blessings,
instead of our cash.

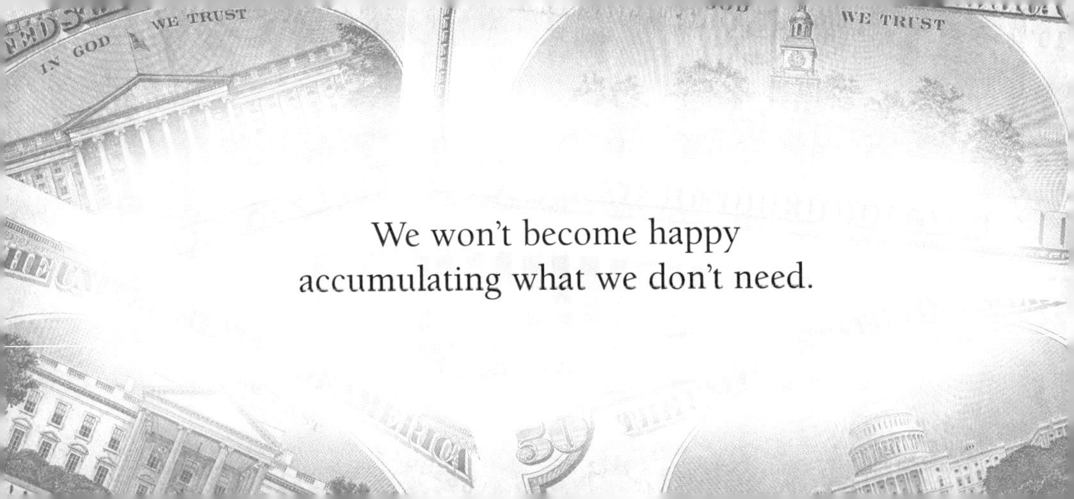

We won't become happy
accumulating what we don't need.

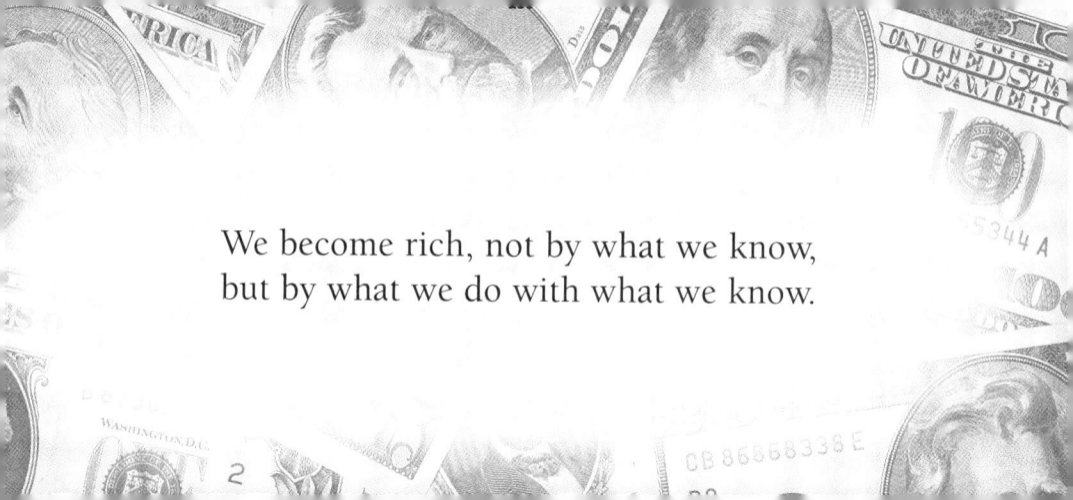

We become rich, not by what we know,
but by what we do with what we know.

A rich life is the reward of courage.

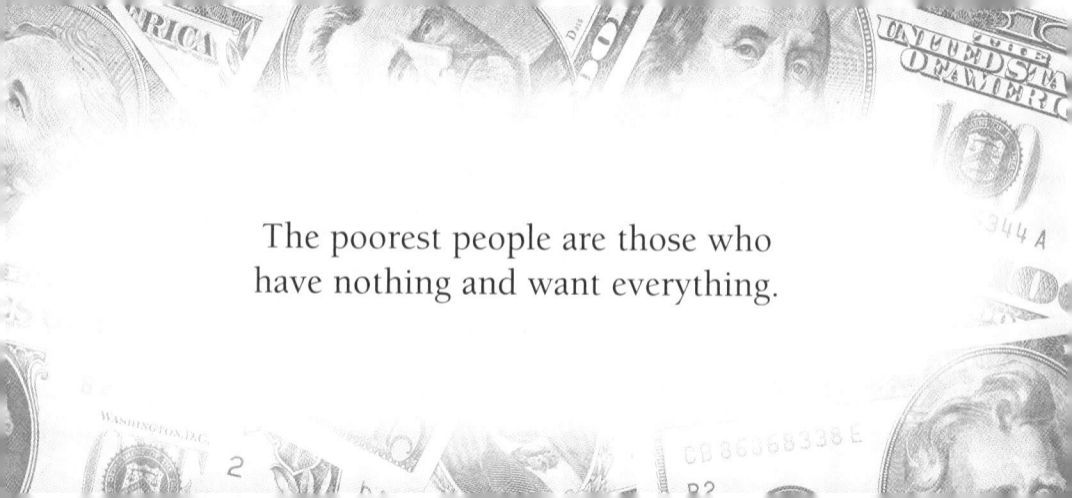

The poorest people are those who have nothing and want everything.

Money is both the cause and the solution of many arguments.

Every life has rich moments.

Money won't keep us happy.

One of the best gifts
we can give our children
is a good example.

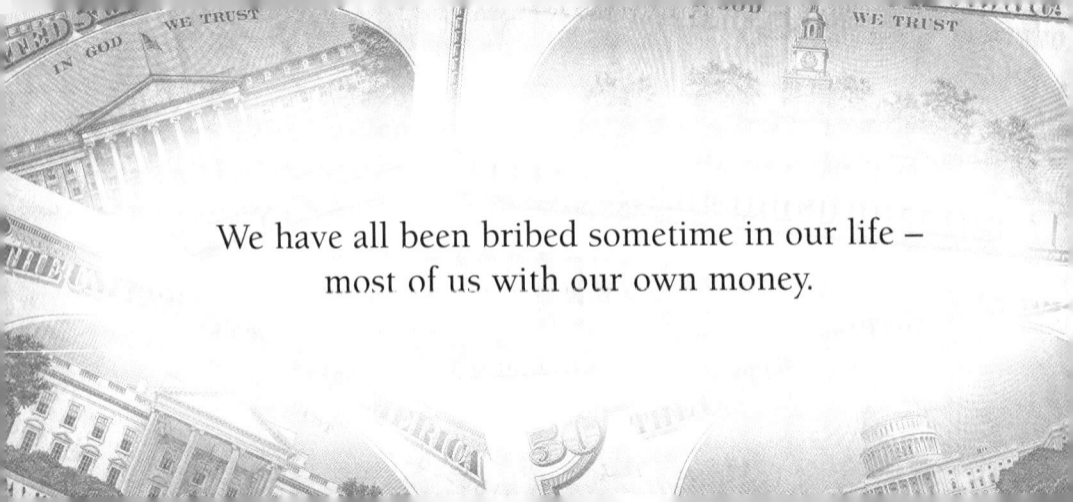

We have all been bribed sometime in our life – most of us with our own money.

Money isn't always worth
what it takes to get it.

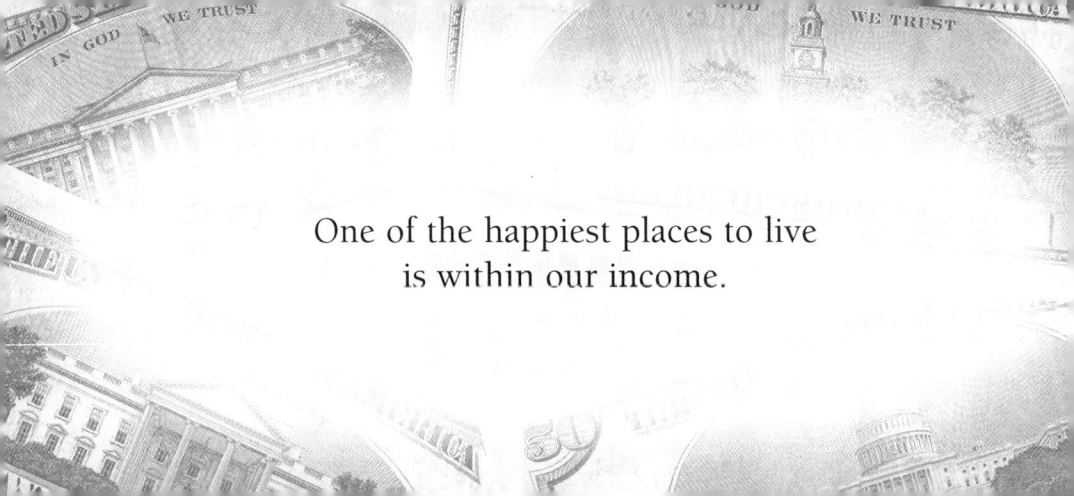

One of the happiest places to live
is within our income.

There are a lot of people
who remain poor
because they act rich.

The greatest wealth
is a clean bill of health.

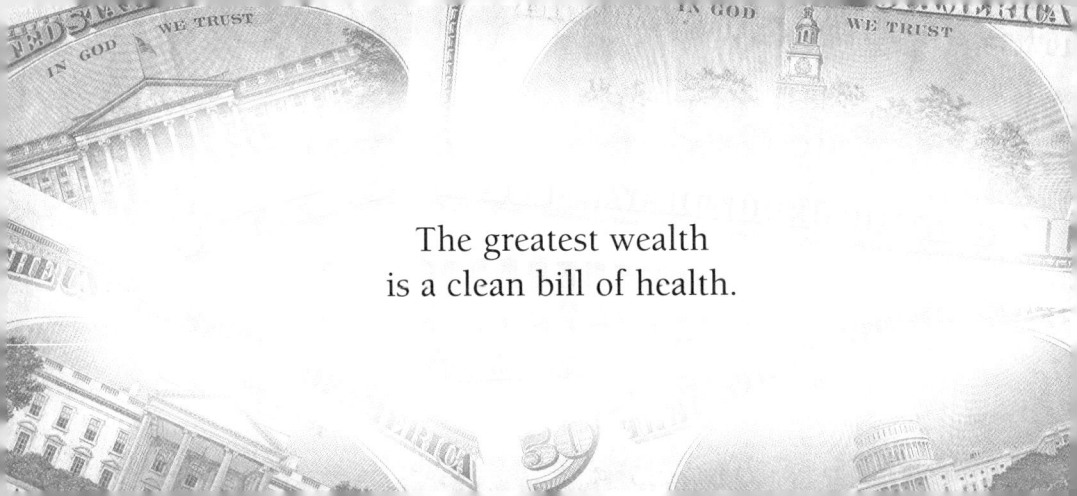

One way to fill our heart
is to empty our pockets.

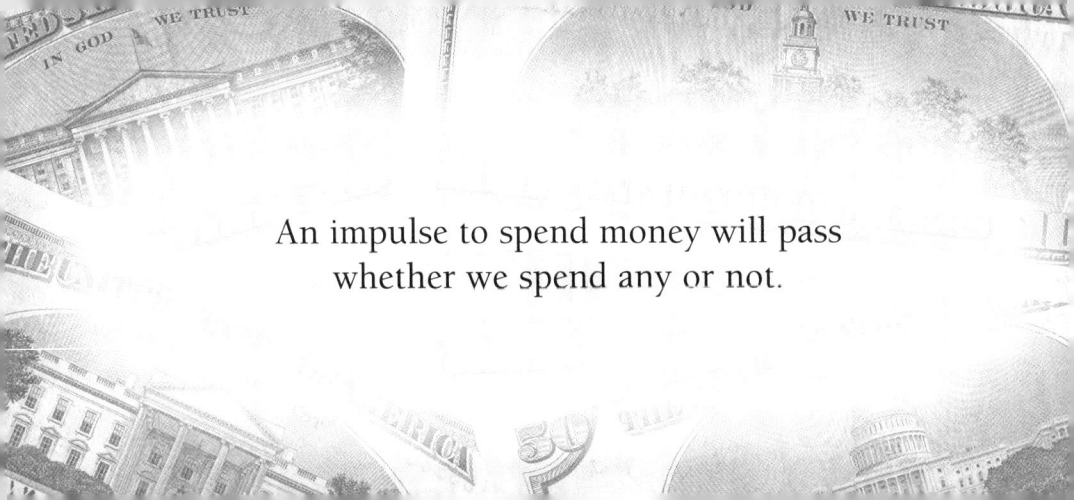

An impulse to spend money will pass whether we spend any or not.

A poor man's problem
is a rich man's opportunity.

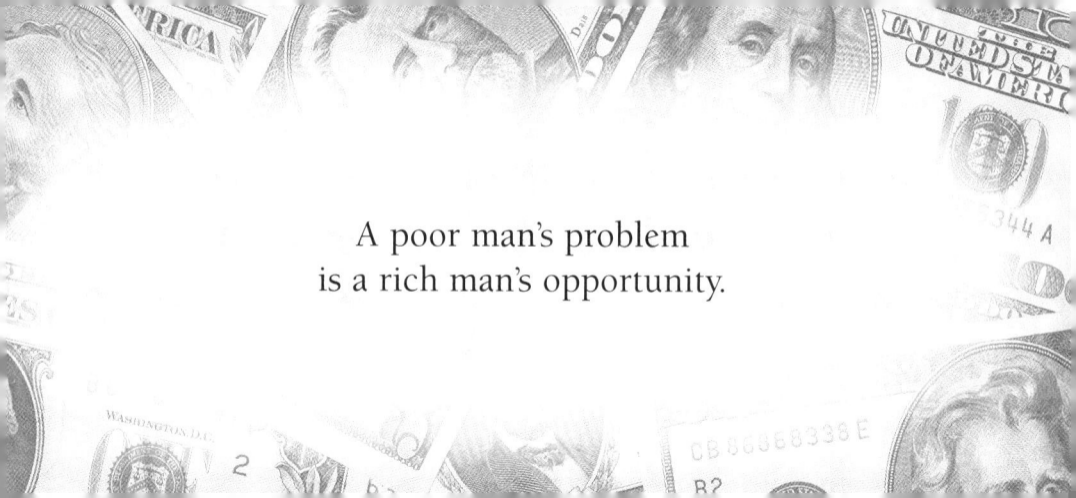

Money is what keeps our desires in check.

The smartest investment
we can ever make
is in ourselves.

Money attracts more flies than honey.

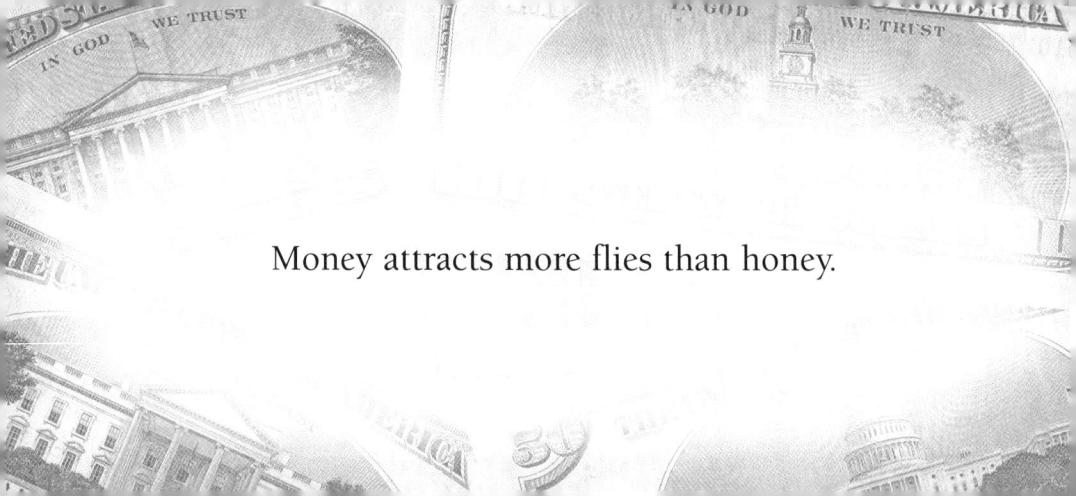

Time is the currency of life.

True expressions of love
don't cost money.

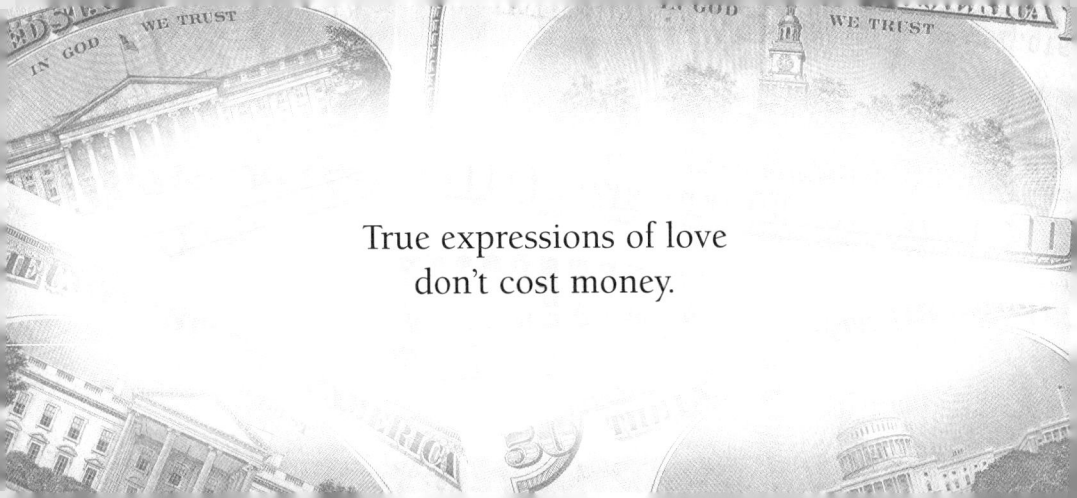

MISER(Y)

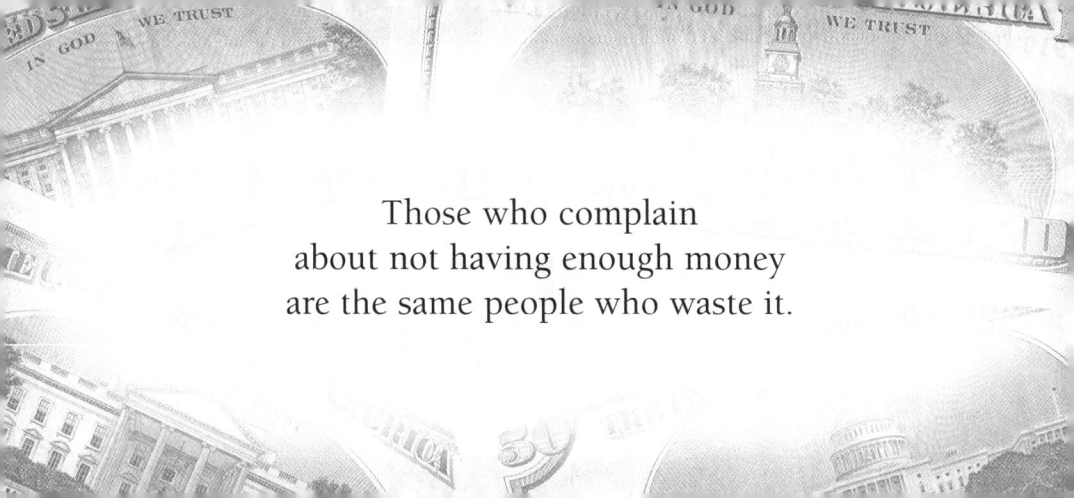

Those who complain
about not having enough money
are the same people who waste it.

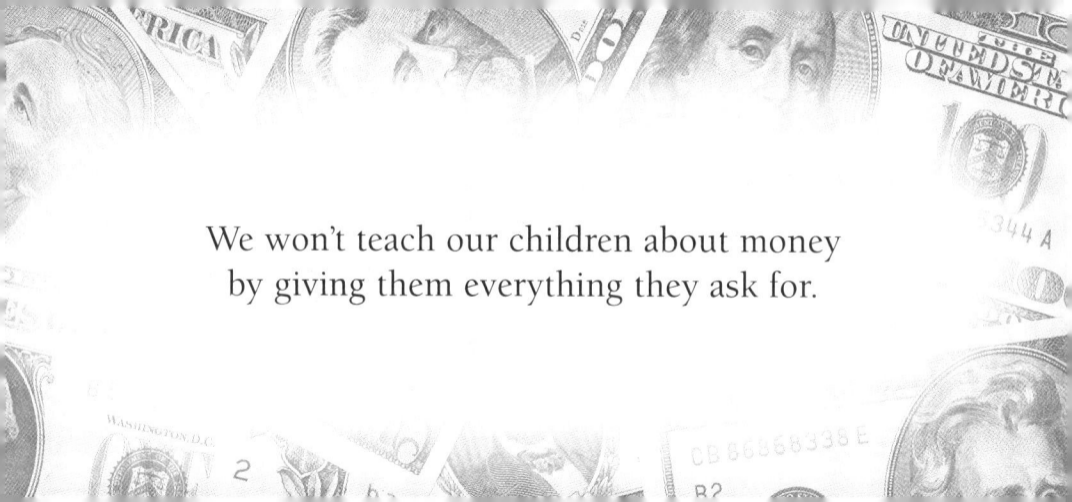

We won't teach our children about money
by giving them everything they ask for.

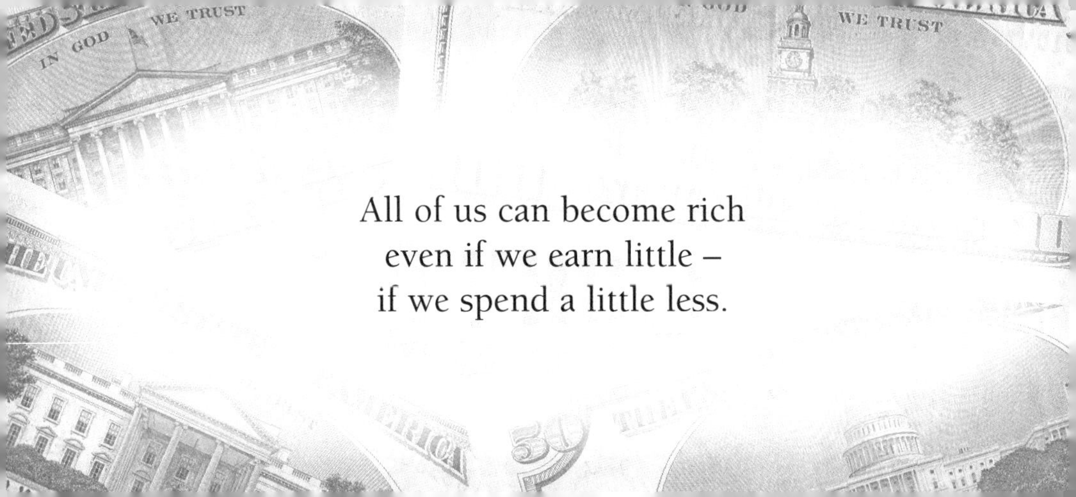

All of us can become rich
even if we earn little –
if we spend a little less.

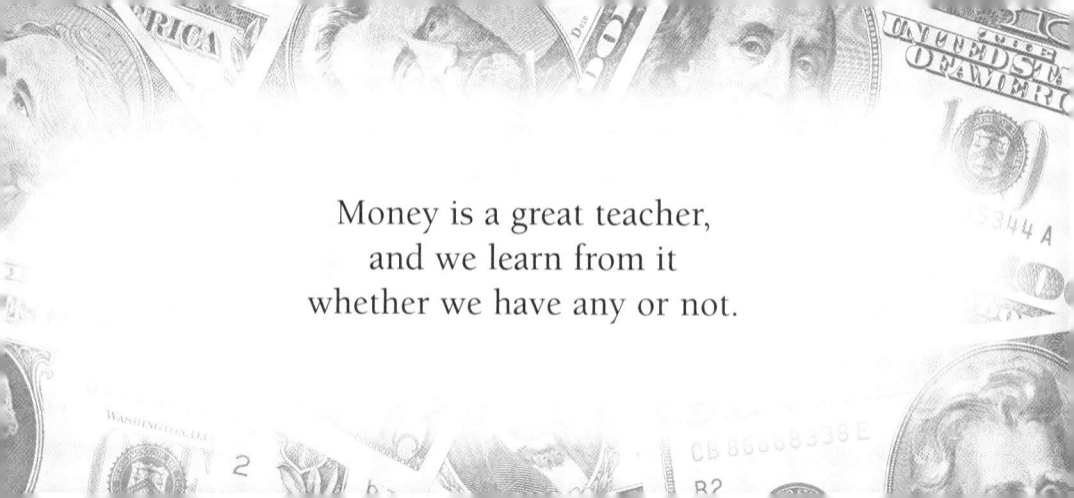

Money is a great teacher,
and we learn from it
whether we have any or not.

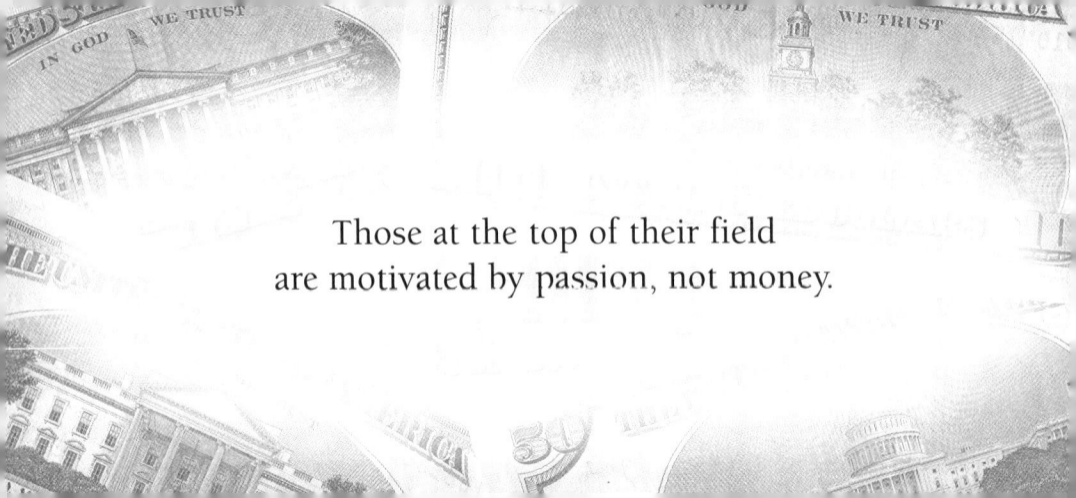

Those at the top of their field
are motivated by passion, not money.

A lot of people think the only way to stop wanting is to have everything.

Worry never made anyone wealthy.

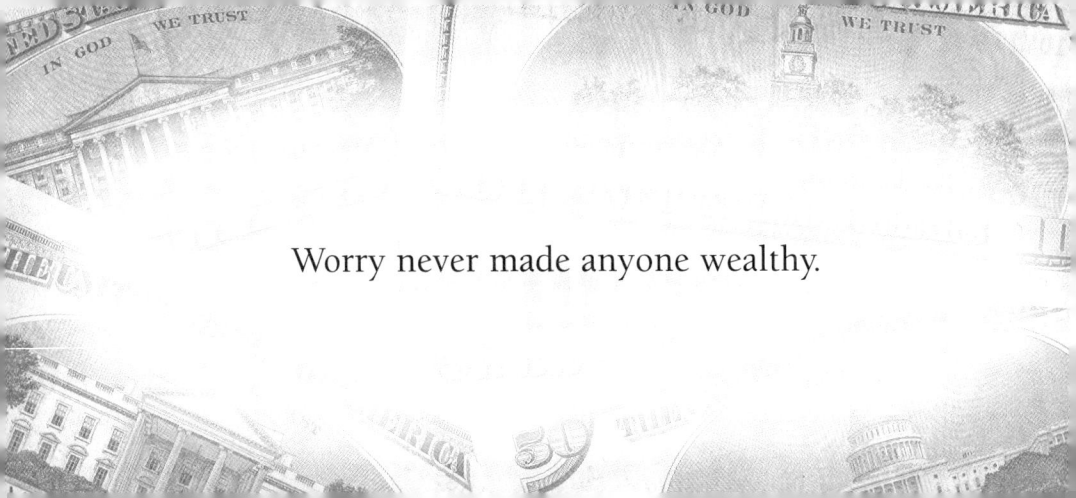

Some people live to work –
others work to live.

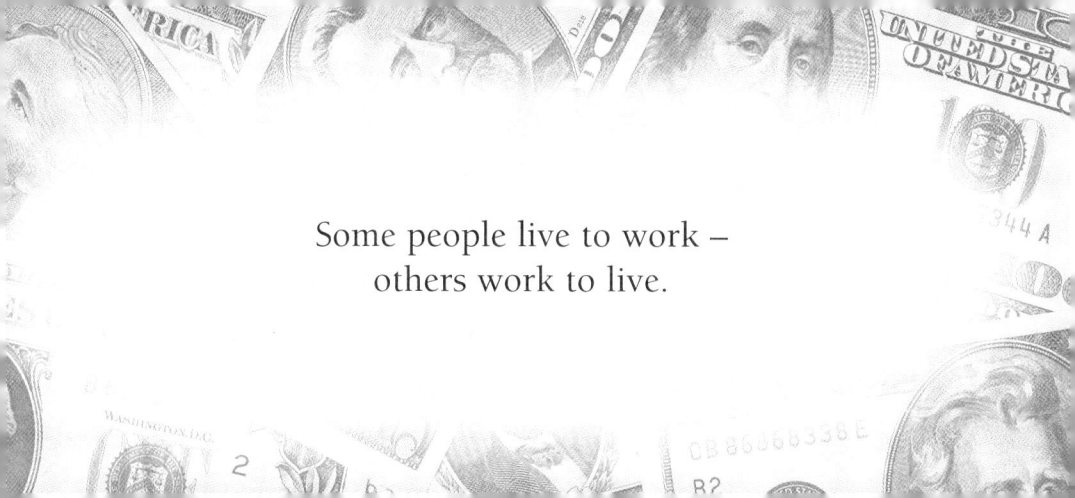

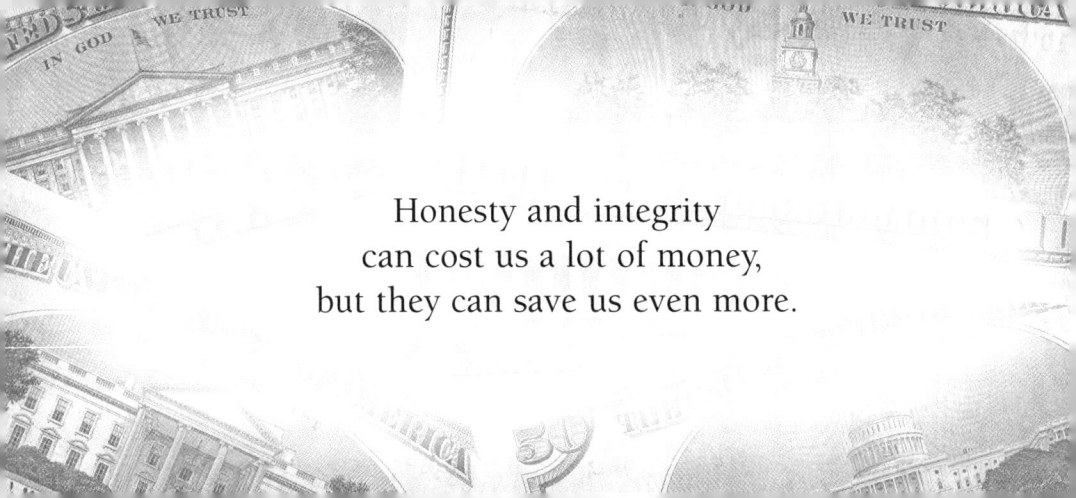

Honesty and integrity
can cost us a lot of money,
but they can save us even more.

PRICE and VALUE
are not always the same.

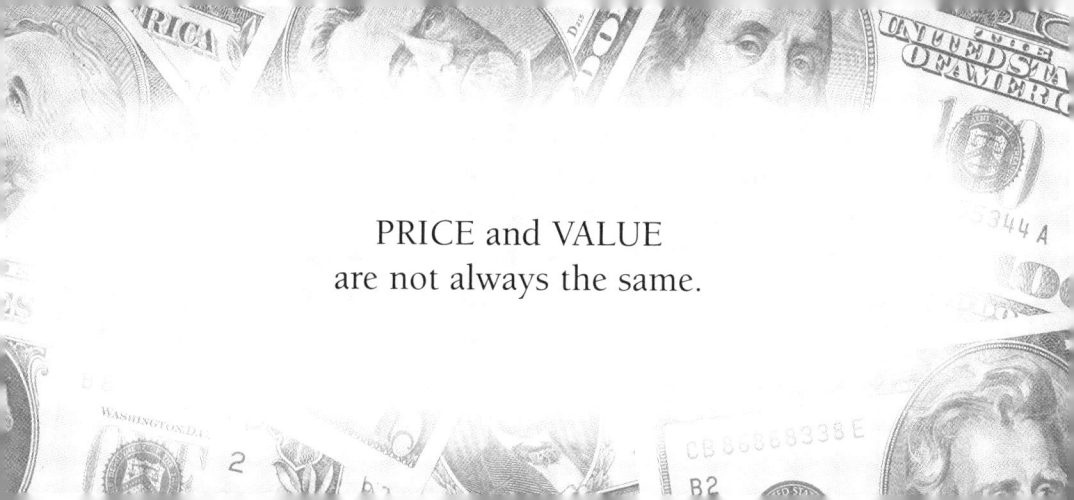

Once we learn enough is enough,
we will always have enough.

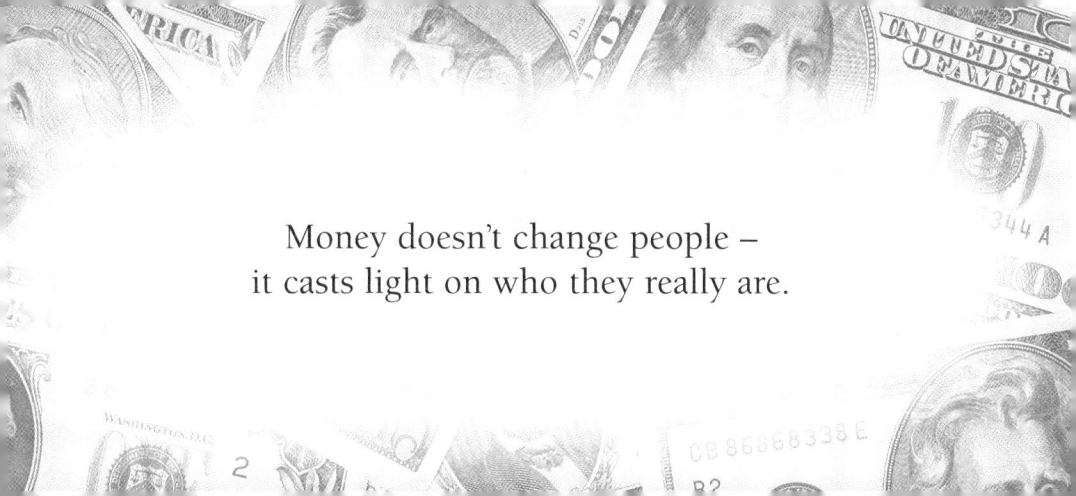

Money doesn't change people –
it casts light on who they really are.

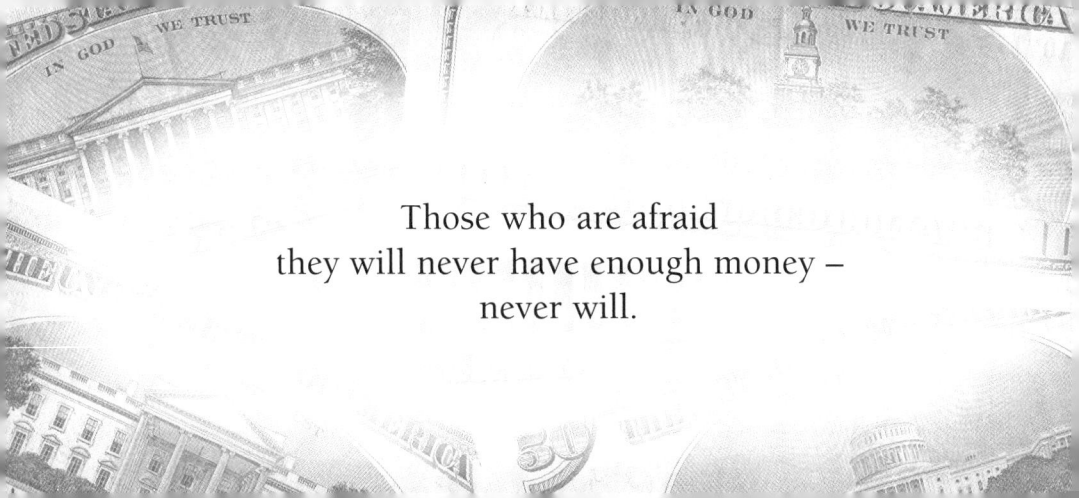

Those who are afraid
they will never have enough money –
never will.

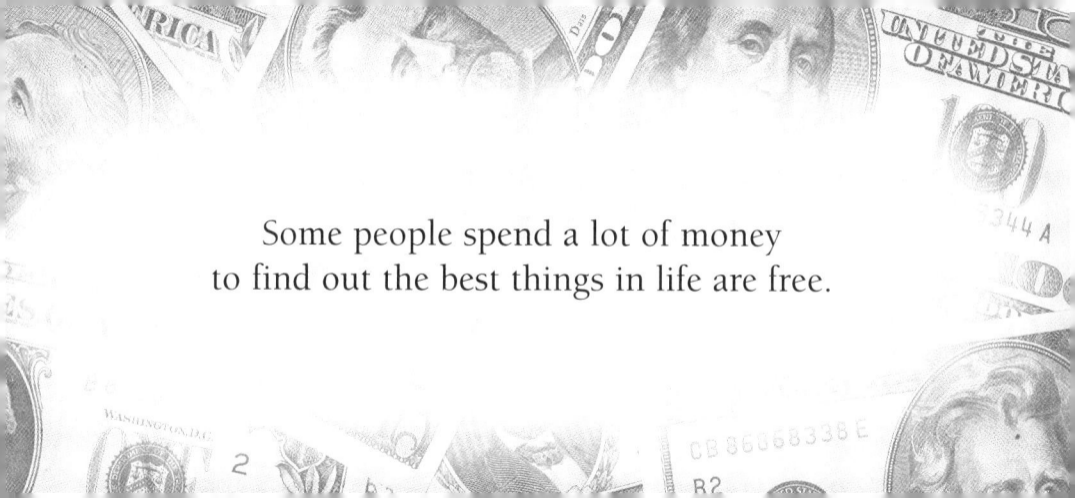

Some people spend a lot of money
to find out the best things in life are free.

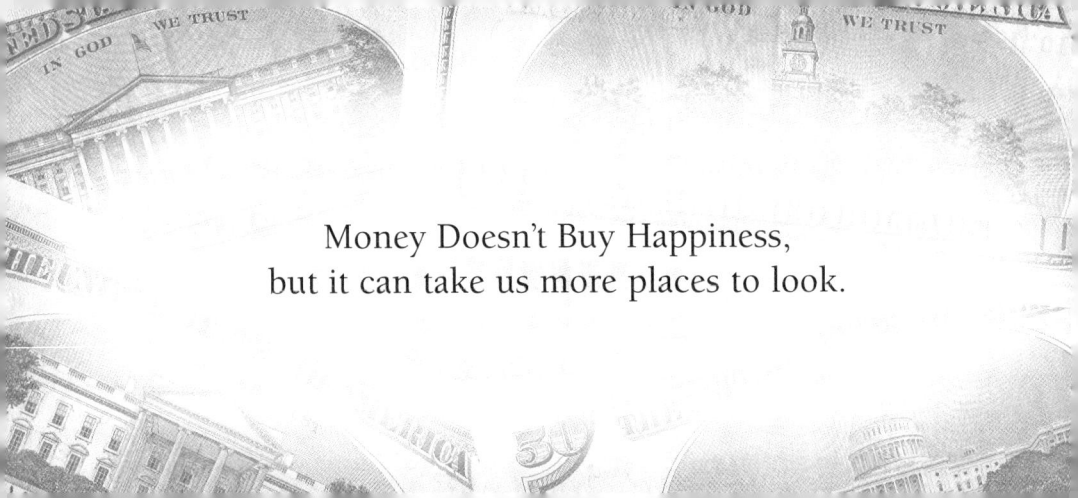

Money Doesn't Buy Happiness,
but it can take us more places to look.

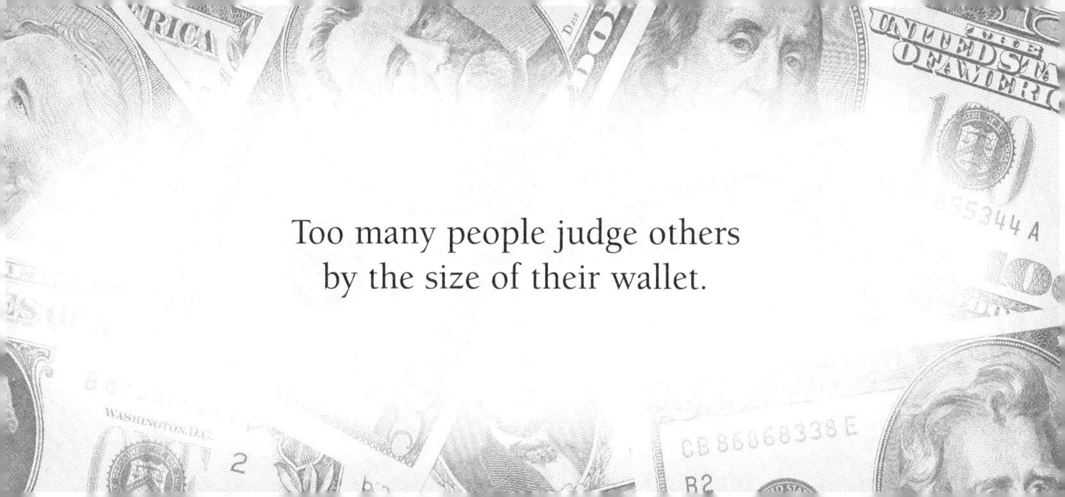

Too many people judge others by the size of their wallet.

When money talks –
virtue walks.

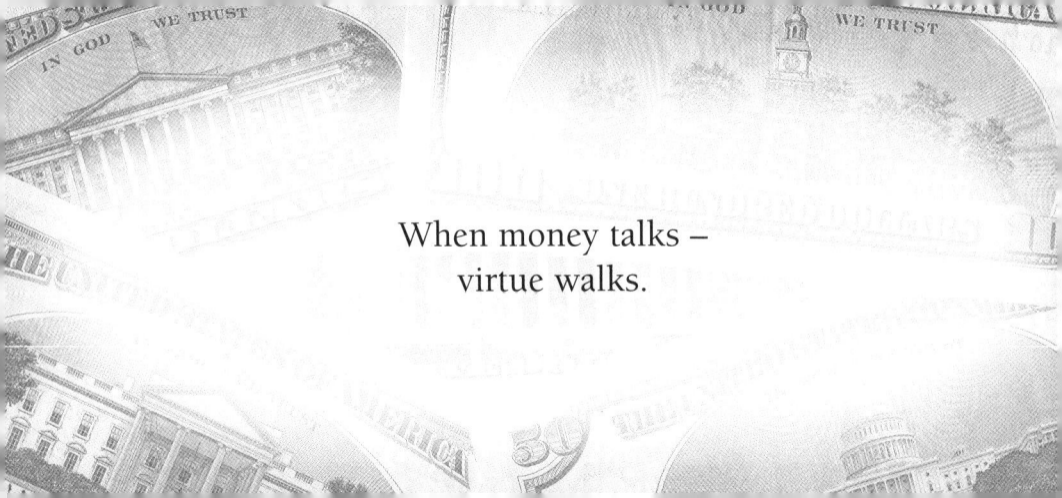

Pleasure can be purchased – happiness can't.

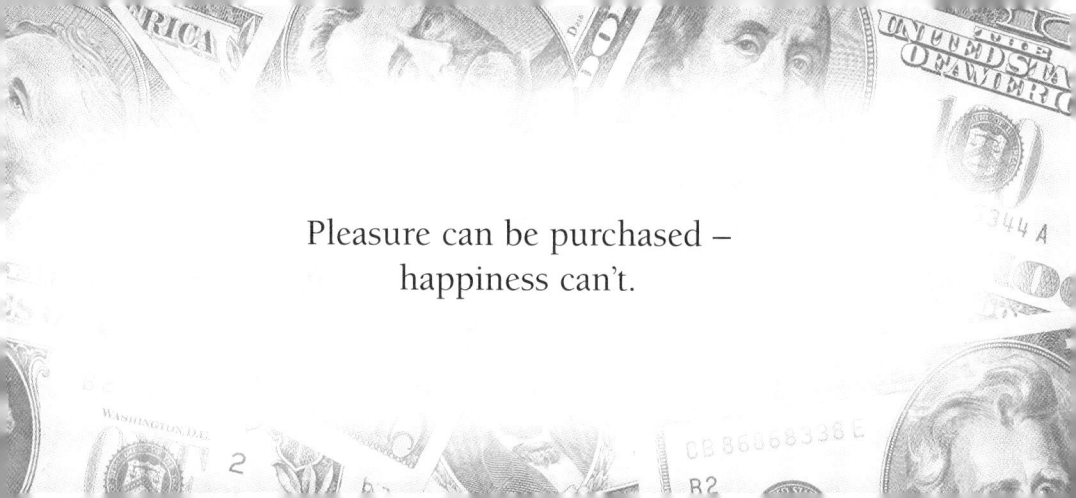

Real wealth is not measured by money, but by our level of happiness.

Giving someone a compliment
will last a lot longer
than giving them money.

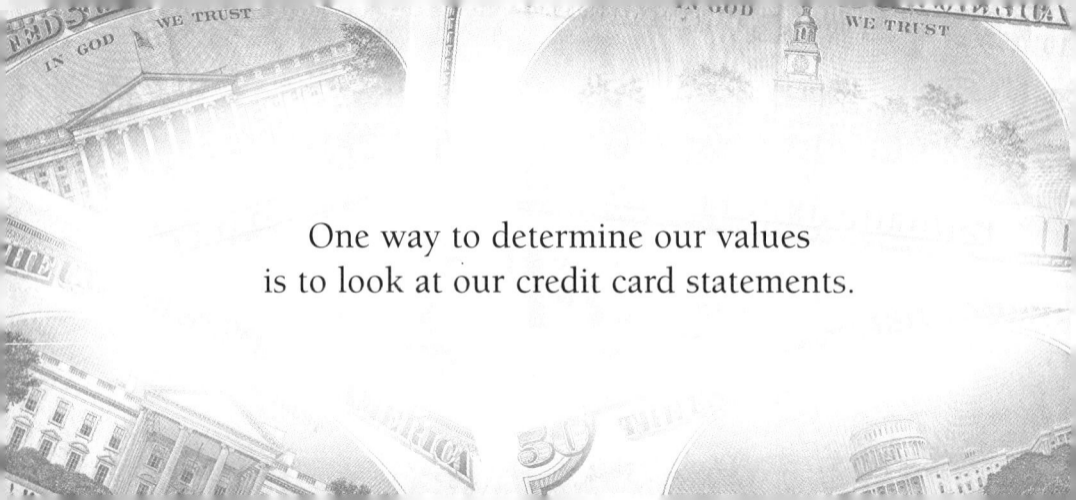

One way to determine our values
is to look at our credit card statements.

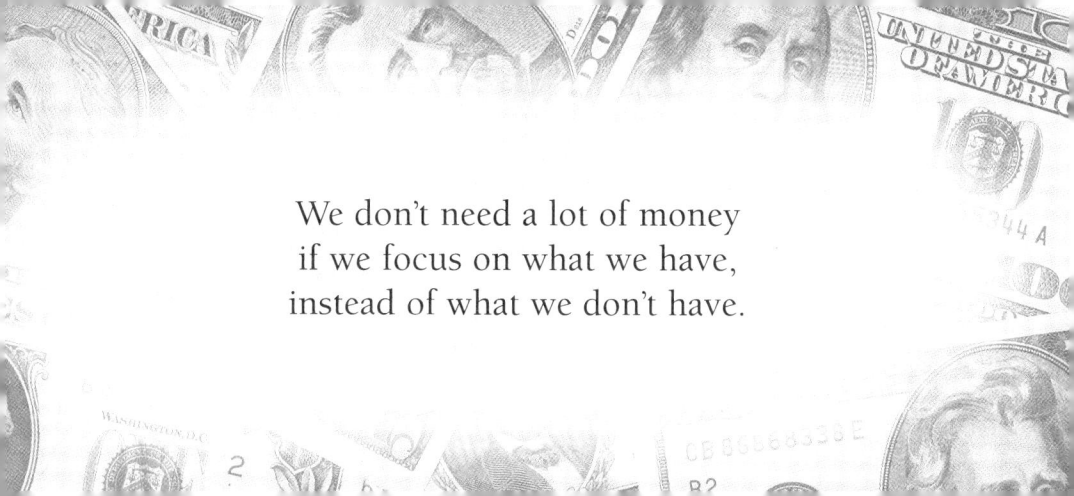

We don't need a lot of money
if we focus on what we have,
instead of what we don't have.

The meaning of our life is realized,
not by what we get,
but by what we give.

Money Doesn't Buy Happiness
because what makes us happy
has no price.

ACKNOWLEDGEMENTS

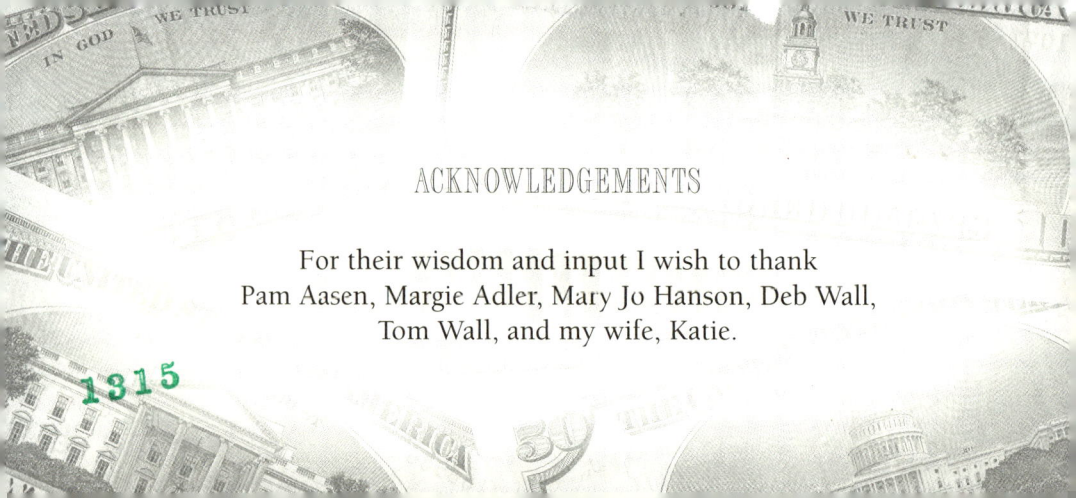

For their wisdom and input I wish to thank
Pam Aasen, Margie Adler, Mary Jo Hanson, Deb Wall,
Tom Wall, and my wife, Katie.

NORMANDALE COMMUNITY COLLEGE
LIBRARY
9700 FRANCE AVENUE SOUTH
BLOOMINGTON, MN 55431-4399